Poems About Her

By: Malvina Mcneill

For anyone who has felt alone in a room full of friends …

Temporary Love

My temporary love

She's so clever

Keeps me hanging on by a thread

Whispers in my ear till my face is red

She's all in my head finishing sentences I never said

My temporary love comes and goes

She's quite the pro at not letting her feelings show

Lingering

Let's linger like low notes in the pits of ones throat

Let's be exclusive with a love that's elusive

Never too intrusive

Let's bow out of the deadliest drought and vow to please each other from here on out

Let's watch a relationship sprout without an ounce of doubt

Let me show you why they call me the zodiac killer

You'll scream all night it's quite a thriller

All I want is to be near you

I don't think I can make it any clearer

There's not a thing I hold dearer

Don't Hide

Please don't hide what I see inside

Show the world your strengths share your spirit

It's quite intense

Please don't hide your gifts at my expense

I want the world to see the person who couldn't love me

Show them more than the ugly

Help them understand why I neglected the plan

Please don't hide

Show the world what it's like to be on your team

I want the world to know where I got my low self esteem

All About

Does she love me?

Does she not?

Dying to know but scared to find out

Living in a drought this is what our relationship is all about

This experience is so enticing bringing flavors sweeter than icing

I'm ignoring all my friend's advice

I don't know where it's going to take me

I just pray you don't break me and make this crazy chemistry just a memory

Searching

I was searching so hard for you

The real you

That I lost myself and everything else

An even though that was no fault of your own

I made it seem so for no reason other than when things go wrong I need someone to blame

Although you weren't as bad as I deemed that's how I made it seem

I apologize endlessly for painting you as a savage

We all do dirt and cause some hurt

I just hope you aren't an expert

Addicted

I'm addicted to women

Can such a sin be forgiven?

So pretty and perfect hell is almost worth it

I try to fight this feeling with spiritual healing but my dreams I end up killing

The obsession is progressing

I never seem to learn my lesson

My love ones are ashamed and I'm to blame

I can sense the tension and feel the rejection

I try to leave it alone but just like a predictable addict

I'm right back it

An worst of all I can't tell if I've made any progress at all

I build myself up to watch myself fall

Lady Love

The lower the lows, the higher the highs

I'd give anything to look into your eyes

You are the cause of my fire

I hope these lines live to inspire

I swear I'm being led by some higher power

I checked the date this love will not expire

You're so intoxicating

I can feel you when you're not even near

This is an experience I don't want to share

Maybe I'll keep it to myself like selfish person with wealth

Love Again

Will I ever Love again?

Let my guard down let pleasure in

Will my future leave me high and dry?

Move on and never explain why

Will my future hold brighter days while I hide from the rays?

Letting life pass me by

Do I dwell for what seems to be an eternity hide what this pain has done to me?

Will I grow hungry for more with an appetite you can't ignore?

Will I ever learn to listen with my ears and not my heart and to open my mouth in order to be heard?

Will I learn to live before the end of this life and I'm dead?

All I See

If you're done saying you're done then why are you still here?

If I'm not the one why am I still here?

You make an appearance several times a year

All I see is a sex addict with self-esteem issues

Tell me who gave them to you

How can you be so successful and lonely?

No friends not even one homie

I see pass the glitz and glam it's all a sham

Deep inside you know you've lost the battle and happiness has left you in its shadows

Sinking

I never thought being there for you would be a promise I couldn't keep

We were so shallow I never imagined it getting so deep

At one point we were completely in sync

We didn't give a damn what the world would think but that ended in a blink of an eye

Soon I was alone on what seemed like a ship it rocks from side to side

The air seemed so thick

I swear I was sinking

So I jumped overboard

I don't know what I was thinking

Burnt Bridges

Don't burn bridges then expect me to send a boat

We were once filled with such hope

Now we struggle to stay afloat

I wish it could been different

A situation far more fitting

You were so persistent

Now the only option is love from a distance

Left Behind

I'm the chance you didn't take the mistake you wouldn't make

I'll be the girl you remember the one with the big heart

The one who thought the world of you

The one that will forgive you

I only wished to give your heart a home but it continues to roam and…

I'm left all alone

Body Language

You walk by without saying a word

Body language is all that can be heard

Swaying your hips and licking your lips

Look my way

Let me see just a glimpse

Damn this girl is intense

Your eyes tell a tale of hardships, laughter and happily ever after's

I can feel your passion burning

If there's a lesson to be taught

I'm learning

Something about you says pain is your virtue but most things don't hurt you

Your aura screams "strong" but doesn't everyone need someone to lean on?

How do I know this?

You can only walk by for so long

As We Lay

As we lie gazing at the stars naming ours

I begin to count the reasons for believing I'm the one you'll be needing each and every season

I want to make your nights brighter than your days in each and every way

Society say's two women shouldn't but they simply don't understand the situation at hand

When you're feeling low you should know the safe place where your heart can go

I'll be waiting when the world has left you shaken

Hand in hand tears streaming

Without love life has no meaning

No one wants to be alone but that's likely the rode I'll choose if it isn't you

As we lie you repeatedly look over your shoulder at a past much colder

I'm reminded that I'm not your first and I won't be your last

Let's

Let's show the world we aren't impossible to love

Let's show the world there's more to life than diamonds and pearls

It's about your head spinning it's about your heart throbbing

The perfect team Batman & Robin

Love

Love so strong it heats up and boils over like lava

Love so hot....over thousands degrees

Love this hot will surely bring to your knees

Love so strong it can lock you up or set you free

Love so strong you are now a part of me!

Have you suffered yet?

If you haven't paid your dues you'll drown in debt

No love will not let the collectors forget

Sweet humble love embrace me don't let the shadow of heartache grace me

Changing

I'm changing for the worst and I swear it hurts

Cutting myself off from the world

I can't stand a soul

You withhold the love that makes me feel whole

You're so cold and all I want is what you promised
a love that's so rare and honest

I wear the most beautiful smile but it only last a while

You're killing me and I'm thinking of killing you

If only they made caskets for two

Feel My Pain

I want you to feel my pain

Feel the depression pulse through my veins

Let the despair run over you

Let it leave you bare naked

If only for a second

I want your insecurities put on a shelf for everyone to see

All courtesy of me

Let the flood gates open with valves that are broken

Bruised

Cripple and corrupted living with a heart that's ruptured

All the scars are visible on my skin but you're still ignoring the state I'm in

When you were mine I could see the darkness shine

Now I live empty and in doubt your love I have to go without

Hate Me

I remember I couldn't breathe I fell to my knees

How could this happen to me you beat your love into my heart and watched it tear me apart

I think you truly hate me the way you berate me

Nothing nice to say to day?

"I'm fat, I'm short and a terrible sport"

You're worse than I thought

Seems to me you need more help than I could offer and even a dope author couldn't tell our love story if it never happen

You Chose Me

Most of the time I feel like crying yes this is what your love do

I didn't choose you chose me

So why now that I set myself free is it all about me?

Let me go is what I shout

Haven't I been through enough you of all people know my life was tough?

I never was good enough

I can't imagine how in my mind I perfected everything you requested

Sometimes I wonder if I was too good and you were all bad

Oh it couldn't be there's no way someone so evil could be a part of me

How did I fall straight into your hell?

You're a master manipulator who lies cheats and steals

What goes around comes around and soon you'll know how it feels

Fresh Air

I need a breath of fresh air

I need you near

I stare at the wall hoping you'll appear but you don't

You're out in the world without a care

What about me?

I don't don' even cross your mind but you rarely leave mine

When will it be our time?

I count the years by seconds it'll take me to except the fact my heart you'll keep breaking

If you had an ounce of empathy you wouldn't have done this

How many chances were there to let me walk freely branch out see what life has to offer me

You say it's just bad timing but I say you don't know the difference between a rock in a diamond

Simple

I'm a simple girl I don't ask for much

Just a good friend to come thru in the clutch

Someone to tell me I'm appreciated and such

Instead you blindfold me and invite me in

I'm being spread so thin

I never asked to be led astray

Your love games leave me in disarray

Surrounded by darkness I'm bound to become it

Is this what you wanted?

To make my sunshine stray

Is that what it takes to make you stay?

Call me a fool but a black cloud is minuscule to life without you

I'll sacrifice my light if it's you I get to hold on to at night

No Going Back

We crossed the line and there's no going back

All we want is our friendship intact

Did we sacrifice that at the door when you pleaded with me and begged for more?

It seemed like an even trade and not at all a masquerade

If we could turn back the hands of time or simply put "press rewind"

I know we would pump the breaks and ultimately alter our fates

When I See You

I'm always stuck on stupid when we meet as if concrete were around my feet

I can feel every tremor as my heart beats

You smell of my favorite treat

My ears yearn to hear you speak with a voice that's oh so clever and unique

I become fragile like a priceless antique

Don't You Know

Don't you know I'm just a girl?

So small in a world hat's so big

I have all these bad habits and rumor has it God's not having

I wish I could please him but I can't be the best while in the flesh

How can I get to the place where's there no pain when I live in the world of sin?

There's a hollow hole inside my heart one I wish to fill

God willing I'll do so with thrill

Come & Go

You come and go in my life so carefree

I wonder if you've taken a second to see what it's done to me

Probably not

Club to club looking for a new hot spot

When you go out you're so excited

So I ask myself

How come I'm never invited?

Lost & Forgotten

Have you ever felt lost or forgotten and before long bitter and rotten?

Thoughts of suicide coincide with feelings you try to hide this is the ride of a lifetime

I'm driving no passengers though I see a bridge that's the way to go

Staring out the window and all I see is you and what we've been through

Now my adrenaline is pumping and a red light is coming but I'm not stopping or slowing down

I'm almost out of this shitty town!

Let Go Young Love

These fucking scars won't heal and the memories still give me a thrill

We said goodbye but now I'm wondering if it was real

Invincible when I'm with you

Invisible when I need you

Went from a victim to a volunteer

Can you tell me how we got here?

I want us happy together or apart adult life we must start

Let go of teenage romances the girl you always spotted at the school dances and move on

This does require us to be strong but something tells me that's what we've been all along

Holding On

Sometimes we hold on too tight for too long causing unnecessary pain

We hope and pray things won't be the same

Deep down inside the love still lives so we search for a fuck to give but memories can't be erased they'll always be a trace

Letting go for the best because emotions cause distress and I'm already a mess

I rather follow my dreams than have my soul rust like a historic building beams

Untitled

Can't eat

Wont sleep

Extremely resistant

I punish myself for you

I fucking hate that you have bragging rights

You're spreading the word I'm not wrapped too tight

I can't love you unconditionally under these conditions

Sanity missing

All of this cause of some kissing

Fatal Attraction

 I poke stick and even slit but my skin seems so thick

I want your name off of me it's becoming more and more costly

Fatal attraction without the acting laying on the bathroom floor gasping

Blood is everywhere

I want to die

I can't, I won't not because of you you'll bring a date to my funeral

I have to stop the bleeding before my hearts stops beating

I'm throwing up everywhere I can't remember the last thing I've eaten

The room is spinning

If it would just stop moving

Just for a sec

Maybe I could recollect

I wake up with water on my face and a hand removing my clothes and for a second I froze

Then I see the vomit and blood and realized I wouldn't be needing those

I wipe my eyes with hopes of seeing things clearer

I make out a face I hold even dearer and I'm covered with a world of disgrace

This is all your fault all it would of took was a visit or two I didn't ask much of you

I'm wrapped in a towel and put to put to bed

No hospital I refuse

When the news reaches you all you can do is laugh as you learn f my blood bath

Eventually you told me I didn't even love myself and for the first time I knew were telling the truth

The fact the that we were having the conversation was proof

Pack Of Pits

Four walls closing in

My blanket seems so thin

I can hear the wind barking

That's what it sounds like to me

A angry pack of pits ripping and roaring

coming for what's mine

No sleep tonight I presume

First thing in the morning I'll break free and leave this room

Dreamt Of Death

I dreamt of your death and asked myself what it meant

Could it mean that terminal disease was more than a plot to get attention from me?

The thought of losing you fatally messed with me

Time passes and I still find myself asking myself how come when I closed my eyes I visualized your demise

God answered my question and it made perfect sense

He showed me that things that don't breathe could die to

It was the death of my romantic feelings for you

Maybe

The people who judge you are the ones you chase

An my face is simply something you wish to erase

You smother me

Invade my space

Call me selfish and ask where my taste is

No need to insinuate I'll give you the food off my plate

You have my back up against the gate

Maybe this is the beginning of love

I can't wait

Live & Die "Tell Them"

Why do you listen to them when they say stay away from me?

I'd never hurt you why can't I live and die for your love if it's all I've been thinking of

I hurt myself for you hurting me

That's what you all consider crazy the irony

Tell them you'll never be finished with me either

Tell them I'm something to look forward to when you're down and out

Tell them how stubborn and spoiled you are and how you love to pout

Try to telling them the truth from here on out

Teenage Girl Woes

Searching for substance in a world so shallow only to find out that's only half the battle

Feeling like your life is over but the world is telling you it's just begun

Falling in love and then being told you're not the one

These are the things that will make a teenage girl run

When you're young and naïve you look at the TV in awe

Saying that could be me with the nice home where you never feel alone

It's filled with memories and all your enemies would envy

Symptoms Of You

I suffer from substance abuse and my addiction is you

I stay up till my head hurts thinking of ways to make it work

I'm completely out of character I'm going berzerk

I loved whole heartedly with every part of me

No half stepping

Until your tender kisses went missing

I begged for your return

I'd work for it

Teach me something new

I'm willing to learn

My soul ignited and you watched it burn

Ashes to ashes dust to dust I was a fool for thinking this was more than a crush

Tell Me

Tell me I'm great how the anxiety kills you before you see me and you can barely wait

Tell me I'm the best thing in your life and without me things wouldn't be right

Tell me how you lose sleep at night looking my pictures

Counting the freckles on my face cursing anyone that dare takes your place

Tell me how much you want me to stay and just how much you would grieve if I so happened to leave

Please tell me I need to hear just how deep this love is we share

Tell me how you can spot me a mile away and how my smile drives you wild

Tell me I'm all you can see and I'm all the woman the others couldn't be

Tell me you're here to stay and beg me to never change because you like me this way

True

See I was so in love with you and you couldn't stay true

Now you're begging for forgiveness and we can take it there but you have a reputation you like to share

When I hold back you attack

Living with that anger living with pain isn't going to make you change

You pushed me away and still I stayed

Our differences have made it this way

I'll just keeping being the best I can be so when your luck runs out you remember me

Yeah you knew I was special that's why you asked to be with me

I also know you gave up on me and there's no way to put that gently

Mockery

I put in the work but you put in the hurt

The blood sweat and tears

The nightmares were clear as day and dark as night

Can you tell me the difference between tears and rain?

Is there really a difference between being in love and being insane?

Making a mockery of my misery

Look at the science project such finesse and intellect A+ is what you get

Truth Is A Lie

I feel you believe your own lies

A sight for sore eyes but to my surprise your ugly inside

I was a prisoner of my mind doing more than time

Not only did I learn to live without you

I learned to love it to

Can you imagine a life with a love one doubting you?

Street Love

Street love is all I've been thinking of

Scream

Shout put me out street love without a doubt

Ask me back before I even pack

Oh street love why do me like that?

I put my hands around your neck and I swear you better not make a sound

Your eyes roll back and around

I know exactly what's going down

Shake, scratch and push me back

Street love is so real

I tell everyone just how I feel

I lower my fist and give you a kiss and whisper there's no better love than this

My Mouth

My mouth may never speak the words my heart feel

My mouth may never say that I'm empty within but I'm still wearing a grin

My mouth may never say that the road I'm on seems all uphill an the journey lacks thrill

My mouth may never say that my prize possession turned out to be just a High School obsession

My mouth may never say I've given up on love an if I look above the simplicity of the sky might make me cry

Dreams Of A Nightmare

Dreams of a nightmare are what I'd like to share

"Picture this"

Going to sleep with the love of your life and waking up with no one there

Before you can even weep you're in a deep sleep

Dreams of a nightmare always seem to happen here

I close my eyes and there I am face to face with every last one of my fears

There's the girl that gave me hell passing out secrets she swore to never tell

I toss turn and shout but help never comes they get lost in route

Dreams of a nightmare fill me with doubt

Constantly reminding me of everything I have to live without

Luck In love

Some have luck in love in others don't an there's no right way to make the heart feel something it won't

The love I was looking for doesn't exists

 I finally understand this

I have more problems than I could fit in these notes but my for odd reason my heart seen you as the antidote but now I see

The same thing that brought us together tore us apart

 Hurting hearts

I Won't (I Can't)

I won't spend my life surviving off lust and nothing more

I won't spend my life with one foot in and the other out the door

I won't spend my life begging for more and providing less

I won't spend my life being depressed and envying the blessed

I won't spend my life with someone who hurt me to the core on their own quest for more

I won't spend my life chasing people and things that don't want to be caught

I won't spend my life blaming Christ when I never did take his advice

Time

Time is something you never truly tell

You can't tell if it's moving slow or fast or just how much has passed

You can't tell it slow down so maybe this time you can grasp it forge a bond make it everlasting

You can't tell time to speed up time to speed up so your wounds can heal an at last you prevail

Time never stands still and it never will

The End

It's evident that you don't care and this is going nowhere

When you're here I just stop and stare our eyes meet but there's a nothing there

No spark or shine it ends like this every time

As if unconditional love was a crime

The tightest bonds are broken when hurtful words are spoken

True color are showing and negativity has awoken

Rose Bud

Rose bud watch you blossom

Beware of the possums

Beautiful rose bud let me see you blossom

I spotted one from the corner of my eye and the beauty nearly made me cry

I wanted to touch and I did so in such a rush

I watched my flesh bust and my fingers drip with blood

Still so very careful not to get any on you rose bud

Every rose has it's thorn but if you open up a beautiful rose will be born

Rose bud let me see you blossom

A Part Of Me

A part of me wanted to see what it was like to have your heartbroken

A part of me wanted to say the words that usually aren't spoken

A part of me knew it was all pretend and the truth wouldn't come out to the end

A part of me thinks of you constantly

A part of me just wants to talk walk along the shore an nothing more

Soul-mates

There are different types of soul mates if you ask me

Not all bring peace when they meet

As soul mates we get irritated when we feel we have to compete with those who aren't elite

The clash runs deeper than you think

We belittle instead of teach because we know the pinnacles each other can reach

I know what you're thinking aren't soul mates supposed to be completely in sync

Possible but reaching the brink can bring as much beauty as the peak

The Impossible

You can't use my heart as a crutch and then tell me I love you too much

I think I love you just enough

Bruises and crescent bite barks send sparks straight to my heart

I fathomed the impossible

I wanted to love the hurt out of you and for you to love the hurt out of me

Even though these hearts bleed for different reasons

I thought maybe we could care for each other in those seasons

I risked it all for love an I'll do it again because I gained a lifetime friend in the end

My Part

Admitting can be the hardest of all

I'm no angel and I play victim quite well

I'm also quite cranky everyone can tell

I have a funny way of showing I care so it's understandable if for a while you didn't believe the feelings were there

I to can take responsibility for my role in it or demise or fall

I know it took long but I was procrastinating that's all

Mind F**k

Just my luck I've been mind fucked

Completely lost and afraid

Your intellectual touch makes me bust

A rare form of lust is the mind fuck

Everything you touch will turn to dust in the name of lust

You want it to pass but don't want to rush you put up a fight and fuss

A rare form of lust is the mind fuck

After

Baby I weathered the storm and I didn't have to

Every time you walked away I lit the path for you

No I wasn't happy about your departure

but what can I do if your no longer caught up in the rapture

Oh lover I wish I could of fell faster but my ego couldn't stand the laughter

Funny How That Works

Sometimes I feel as though I was a disappointment and you regret the role you appointed me

An even though we don't converse daily

I see you in nearly everything I do and wonder if you know it's all thanks to you

You challenged me to see things differently and these are the type of things that stick with me

You encouraged me to let go of pass pains and leave alone things I can't explain

This is a few of many reasons why when I hear your name I'm not ashamed

For the most part the good outweighs the bad and I'm grateful for what we had